WEST GERMAN
FOOD AND DRINK

Barbara Einhorn

The Bookwright Press
New York • 1989

FOOD AND DRINK

British Food and Drink
Caribbean Food and Drink
Chinese Food and Drink
French Food and Drink
Greek Food and Drink
Indian Food and Drink
Italian Food and Drink
Japanese Food and Drink

Jewish Food and Drink
Mexican Food and Drink
Middle Eastern Food and Drink
North American Food and Drink
Russian Food and Drink
Southeast Asian Food and Drink
Spanish Food and Drink
West German Food and Drink

First published in the
United States in 1989 by
The Bookwright Press
387 Park Avenue South
New York, NY 10016

First Published in 1988 by
Wayland (Publishers) Ltd.
61 Western Road, Hove
E. Sussex BN3 1JD, England

© Copyright 1988 Wayland (Publishers) Limited

Typeset by Lizzie George, Wayland
Printed in Italy by G. Canale & C.S.p.A., Turin

Library of Congress Cataloging-in-Publication Data

Einhorn, Barbara
    West German food and drink / by Barbara Einhorn.
      p. cm. -- (Food and drink)
    Bibliography: p.
    Includes index.
    Summary: Describes, in text and illustrations, the food and
beverages of Germany in relation to its history, geography, and
culture. Also includes recipes and information about regional
specialities and festive foods.
    ISBN 0-531-18232-0
    1. Cookery, German–Juvenile literature. 2. Beverages–Germany
(West)–Juvenile literature. 3. Germany (West)–Social life and
customs–Juvenile literature. [1. Cookery, German. 2. Germany
(West)–Social life and customs.] I. Title. II. Series.
TX721.E36 1989
394.1'2'0943- -dc 19
                                                    88-23318
                                                        CIP
                                                        AC

Contents

West Germany and its people

West Germany is the largest of several German-speaking countries in Central Europe. It has a population of 61 million, spread over an area of 250,000 sq km (96,500 sq mi). The landscape varies greatly and so does the way people live.

West Germany slopes gently from the Alps and alpine foothills in the south, through the Central Highlands onto the North German Plain and the flatlands bordering the North and Baltic seas. As a result of this north-south incline, the main rivers in West Germany flow northward and into the North Sea via the Rhine, the Ems, the Weser and the Elbe, which forms the border in the north between West and East Germany.

West Germany has very beautiful areas of forest and mountain, that are

A village nestles on the banks of the Rhine with vineyards on the steeply sloping hills behind it, bare in early spring.

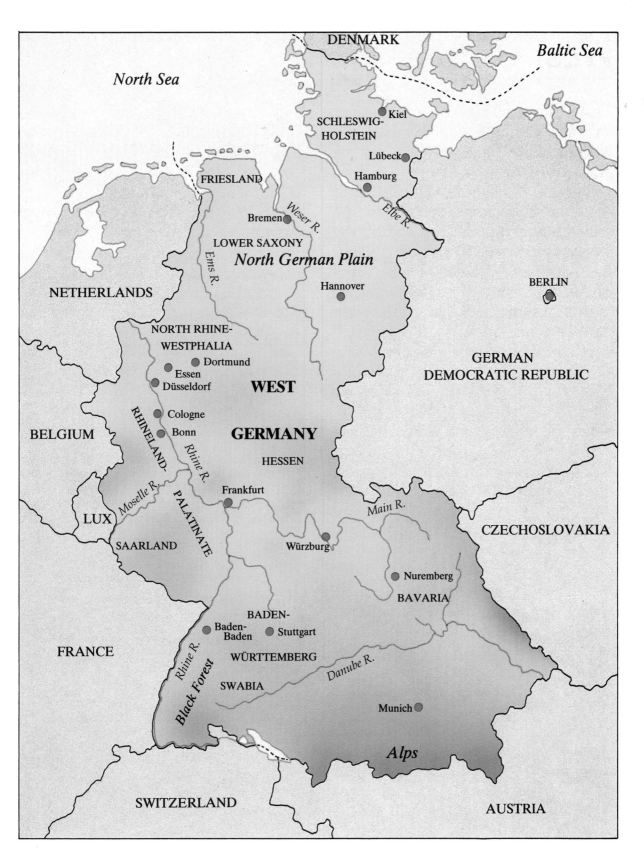

DENMARK

Baltic Sea

North Sea

SCHLESWIG-
HOLSTEIN

● Kiel

Lübeck ●

FRIESLAND

Hamburg ●

Weser R.

Elbe R.

Bremen ●

LOWER SAXONY

North German Plain

Ems R.

NETHERLANDS

Hannover ●

BERLIN ●

NORTH RHINE-
WESTPHALIA

● Dortmund

GERMAN
DEMOCRATIC REPUBLIC

Essen ●
Düsseldorf ●

WEST

RHINELAND-

Cologne ●

Bonn ●

GERMANY

BELGIUM

Rhine R.

HESSEN

Moselle R.

PALATINATE

Frankfurt ●

Main R.

LUX

CZECHOSLOVAKIA

SAARLAND

Würzburg ●

● Nuremberg

BAVARIA

BADEN-

FRANCE

Baden- ●
Baden

● Stuttgart

Rhine R.

WÜRTTEMBERG

Danube R.

Black Forest

SWABIA

Munich ●

Alps

SWITZERLAND

AUSTRIA

5

loved by tourists, such as the Black Forest and Bavaria, with its lakes and mountain chalets. But the Central Upland valleys and parts of the huge flat plains in the north are neither well known nor are they densely populated. In contrast, the Ruhr industrial area with its cities Düsseldorf, Dortmund, Essen and Cologne, which all run into one another, supports 9 percent of the entire population on only 2 percent of the country's area.

One in three West Germans lives in a large town or city of more than 100,000 inhabitants. Yet many West Germans still prefer to escape hectic city life, and one in twelve lives in a village with a population of fewer than 2,000.

West Germany is a republic known as the Federal Republic of Germany (FRG) and is divided into 10 states, or *Länder*. It is bordered today by nine other countries, and there are no natural land barriers to the north, west or east. Its geographical location has meant that throughout its history, Germany has been a region of migration and shifting borders, bringing together many peoples with different ideas and cultures.

West Germany's geographical location in Central Europe has also been a factor in the many political clashes and wars in which the Germans have been involved, from the time of the Holy Roman Empire in the tenth century to World War II (1939-45).

The four Allies who defeated Germany in World War II – France, Britain, the Soviet Union and the United States – were determined that Germany should never again be in a position to unleash a war. With this aim in mind, they divided the country into four zones, each administered by one of the Allies. In 1949, the three western zones became the Federal Republic of

Most West German cities have a pedestrian mall, like this one in Baden-Baden, the famous spa town in the beautiful Black Forest.

An aerial view over the houses and parks of West Berlin looking east from Witzleben station, with East Berlin in the distance.

Germany, while the Soviet zone became East Germany, or the German Democratic Republic (GDR), with a population today of 18 million living on 108,000 sq km (41,698 sq mi). Berlin, the former capital city, was also divided into four. East Berlin is today the capital of the GDR; West Berlin is regarded as part of the Federal Republic, but is still legally under the control of the three Western Allies – France, Britain and the United States.

West Germany has large resources of coal and minerals, which have laid the basis for its steel, chemical and engineering industries. It is one of the world's leading industrial nations and an influential member of the European Economic Community (EEC). However, there are some problems. West Germany's famous car industry is facing competition from Japanese cars, and recession on the world market has thrown 3 million people out of work. The Ruhr area, the center of German industrialization in the 1920s and 1930s, and heart of the West German "economic miracle" of the 1950s and 1960s, is one of the worst-hit areas, with one in four people out of work.

German food and drink reflects the great variety of cultural influences on Germany's history, and is remarkably different from the stereotype of stodgy food often associated with Germany. This book will concentrate on the food and drink of West Germany, and will not include in detail the eating

West Germans like to make the most of their short summers by eating outside, like the people at this restaurant in Dortmund.

and drinking habits of East Germany, Austria or Switzerland. Even within West Germany, we shall find there is a great deal of regional variation, reflecting historical and geographical differences. And since we tend to think of West Germany as a country that exports high-quality industrial goods, we may be surprised to discover that it is the world's fourth largest agricultural exporter. In fact, West Germany exports more food and drink than it does iron, steel or textiles.

Agriculture

Geographical differences have had a marked influence on the foods of the various regions. For example, West Germany's only coastline is in the north, so fishing, and consequently fish dishes, are extremely important in Friesland and Schleswig-Holstein. Similarly, the great North German Plain lends itself to crop growing, unlike the more mountainous regions of the south. Grains, cereals and potatoes are grown in Lower Saxony, and sheep and cows graze on the marshy, reclaimed land behind the sea dikes of Schleswig-Holstein. A lamb roast at Easter has always been a delicacy in Germany, because it is only in the north that sheep are farmed. Pork is the cheapest meat in West Germany, but lamb is the most expensive.

The type of food grown can also be influenced by economic and social change. The potato has always been the staple food of the Germans. However, with the increased affluence since the *Wirtschaftswunder* (the "economic miracle") of the 1950s and 1960s, the potato has become less important in the West

Fish being unloaded in the early morning light in Bremerhaven. From the boat they will be taken straight to the fish markets.

German diet. So there are now far more grain and cereal crops grown for animal feed on the North German Plain than there are potato crops. Pig farming is widespread in the northern and western parts of the country, especially in Lower Saxony and Westphalia. Other meats have become much more important with the change in the German diet from the stereotype of sausages and *Sauerkraut*. There are many poultry farms, and cattle graze in the rolling Central Uplands, as well as on the alpine pastures of Bavaria and the Black Forest.

Animal husbandry accounts for 70 percent of all food production in West Germany. West Germany is very nearly self-sufficient in the

Most German breads are made from rye flour, so this winter wheat in the north of the country will be intended for animal feed.

production of cereals, potatoes, sugar, beef and pork, as well as in dairy products, but has to import most of its vegetables and fruit from the sunnier countries to the south. West German farms tend to be small family farms, and often the farmer has a second job in a nearby town. Although agriculture is important in West Germany, it employs only about 7 percent of all West German workers.

West Germany is the fourth largest producer of meat and dairy products in the world.

In the early spring, sheep graze in the alpine foothills in Bavaria.

Processing the food

Most exported German food is processed. Best known outside the country are German butter and cheese, and, of course, the huge variety of German sausages, ranging from *Leberwurst* (liver sausage) and Bierwurst to *Frankfurters* and *Bockwurst*. German bread is also

Bavaria is the home of an abundance of West German cheese varieties, as you can see from this attractive market stand in Munich.

famous for its variety and its nutritional value. Within the European Economic Community (EEC) only France produces more milk, butter and cheese.

Strict laws govern the production of butter and cheese, and all dairies are inspected regularly, with samples of their milk and butter taken away for testing. In the making of sausages, too, no cereals, coloring or other additives are allowed. Sausages must contain 100 percent meat. Recently, West

Hygiene regulations in West German sausage factories are very strictly followed. All sausages must contain 100 percent meat.

Germany has been forced, by EEC regulations, to accept imports of meat-based spreads and canned meats from other EEC member countries, which do not conform with these stringent standards.

West Germany produces more sausages than any other country in the world – and there are more than 1,500 different types!

Shopping for food

Despite the growth of huge "hypermarkets" as well as supermarkets, Germans still tend to shop daily for fresh produce. This helps to explain why specialty shops have not been eliminated by the supermarket, as they have been in so many other countries. The small corner general store, *"Tante Emma Laden"* (Aunt Emma's Store), where one could buy anything from fresh rolls, flour and tea to buttons, thread, nails and wood, has vanished.

But a daily visit to the baker's for fresh bread or cakes for afternoon coffee, and a stop at the butcher's to see what looks best for dinner, are a must.

The corner store, or Tante Emma Laden, *still offers personal service as well as a very wide range of goods.*

Buying fresh vegetables at the market is fun. The display at this Munich street market is typically colorful and appetizing.

Every town has its municipal street market, where farmers and market gardeners from the outskirts of the town come once or twice a week to sell their fresh produce. The air is filled with the spicy aroma of sizzling hot *Bratwürste* (sausages) frying on a brazier or charcoal grill. The air is filled with the shouts of the vegetable vendors, and the flower stands add an abundance of color to the scene. You can often buy freshly made butter, quark or cheese from a small local producer, too.

Locally produced fresh quark being sold in a suburb of Hamburg. Quark is a soft cheese much used in German cooking.

Zu Tisch! (To the table!)

Frühstück (breakfast)

The day begins early in West Germany, and Germans value a good breakfast to get them going. They eat a variety of breads with cheese, sausage and a choice of honeys and jams. On Sundays breakfast is more elaborate and usually includes fresh rolls and a boiled egg. Coffee is the main breakfast drink, although some people prefer tea, and children usually drink milk or hot chocolate. As a result of American influence in West Germany since World War II, children often eat breakfast cereals such as cornflakes. Fruit juices and yogurt are also popular.

Zweites Frühstück
(second breakfast)

No matter whether they go to work or to school, most Germans will take some *Butterbrote* or *Stullen* (sandwiches) with them for a mid-morning snack. The morning is long, both for children and for working adults: school begins and most offices open at 8 a.m. and the lunch break is not until 12:30 or 1 p.m. So a sandwich is just what is needed to keep energy levels up.

Nicole and Caroline Kleiser, and their visiting Canadian friend, enjoy a chat with their mother over breakfast before cycling to school in Hamburg.

Ice creams and elaborate ice-cream sundaes are very popular throughout Germany. There is a wide choice on the menu of all good cafés.

Mittagessen (midday meal)

The Germans eat their hot main meal in the middle of the day. Since school – except for the *Gesamtschulen* (comprehensive schools) in some West German states – finishes around midday, children generally go home for their dinner. If, however, their parents are out at work, children may go to a *Hort*, a day care center attached to the school, where they will be given a hot meal and can play or do homework until their parents come home.

At the workplace, *Mittagessen* is eaten in the cafeteria or at a local restaurant. Traditionally, the midday meal used to be a thick lentil or potato soup with a *Bockwurst* added. This kind of soup is known as *Eintopf*, as the whole meal is all cooked in one pot. Another favorite with children is *Verlorenne Eier* (lost eggs), which consists of poached eggs on a bed of spinach, eaten with boiled potatoes. *Himmel und Erde* (heaven and earth) is also popular. The name of this dish comes from its ingredients – a tasty mixture of apple (growing up high) and potatoes (growing in the ground), mashed together. Dessert might consist of a compote of fruit, *Eierkuchen* (pancakes) or *Milchreis*, a rice pudding cooked with milk and with raisins and cinnamon added. This is sometimes eaten as a main dish and children love it.

A tasty meal of Himmel und Erde. *Potatoes are mixed with apple to make this popular dish.*

Kartoffelpuffer
(Potato pancakes)

You will need:
2 lb of potatoes
2 eggs
1 onion
1 level teaspoon of salt
oil for frying
lemon juice

What to do:
Peel the potatoes into a bowl of water with a little lemon juice in it to stop the potatoes from turning brown. (1) Grate the potatoes and grate or finely chop the onion. Squeeze the surplus water from the potatoes before mixing in the other ingredients. Heat the oil in a frying pan. (2) When it is hot, drop spoonfuls of the mixture into the pan. (3) Press flat with a spoon and fry until crisp and golden — about 3 minutes on each side. (4) Serve immediately, with *Apfelmus* (applesauce). Safety note: The oil must be very hot so that the fritters don't stick to the pan. Be careful when you put the fritters in, so the oil doesn't spit. Wear an apron and use an oven mitt.

Abendbrot (evening meal)

The family comes together for the evening meal, which is based on different breads and cold meats. A central ingredient is *Aufschnitt*: a selection of cold meats and sausages decoratively arranged on a plate. Dill cucumbers, a salad and various cheeses complete the meal. Most people drink black tea or herb tea at this meal, sometimes with a little dash of rum added on a cold, wintry evening. To follow, there may be a delicious dessert based on quark, a cross between cottage cheese and yogurt.

When you ask a butcher for half a pound of Aufschnitt, *he will give you a selection of sausages and cold meats.*

Marble cake looks like a sculpture and tastes delicious, but in fact it is not difficult to bake.

Aufschnitt
(Cold meat platter)

You will need:
¼ lb of German salami, sliced
¼ lb of German cervelat, sliced
3 oz of Westphalian ham (or other smoked ham), sliced
3 oz of German *Bierwurst*, sliced
3 oz of *Lachsschinken* or *Kassler*, sliced
3 pickles
fresh parsley
1 hard-boiled egg, sliced

What to do:
Roll up each slice of meat and arrange in concentric circles on a large round plate. Decorate with slices of egg, pickles and sprigs of parsley.

Serve with different kinds of German bread such as, *Roggenbrot* (rye bread), *Pumpernickel* or *Vollkornbrot*, (cracked rye and wheat bread) and some salad.

Früchtequark
(quark fruit cream)

You will need:
3 3/4 cups of low fat quark or yogurt, or
   yogurt and cottage cheese, mixed.
1/2 cup of milk
1/2 cup of sugar
5 citrus fruits (oranges, mandarin oranges
   etc)
juice and grated rind of 1 lemon

What to do:
Mix the quark (or yogurt, etc.) with the
milk and sugar until smooth. (1) Add the
lemon rind and juice, and the juice of 2
oranges (or mandarin oranges). (2) Lastly,
fold in the chopped segments of 2 oranges.
Pour into 4–5 glasses or bowls.   (3)
Decorate with the segments of the last
orange. Chill before serving. For a change
you could also use berries or any other
fruits in season in place of the citrus fruit.
Instead of adding milk, for a more festive
occasion use heavy cream. Whip and fold
in at the end with the fruit segments.

Kaffee und Kuchen

Sundays in Germany are very much
reserved for the family. A visit to
aunts and uncles or grandparents for
coffee and cake after a walk in the
woods is almost a ritual event. Some
children complain about this visit,
seeing it as an obligation, but
certainly Germans are famous for the
cakes they bake for this occasion.
The glass display case in any
German café is a tempting sight with
its many varieties of cake for sale.

Marmorkuchen

(marble cake)

You will need:
9 oz (2 sticks + 2 tablespoons) of salted
   butter or margarine
1⅓ cups of sugar
3¾ cups of flour
4 eggs
juice and rind of one lemon
2 teaspoons of baking powder
½ cup of milk
⅓ cup of cocoa
2 tablespoons of sugar
Angelfood cake pan,
   about 19 cm (7") in diameter

What to do:
Cream the butter and sugar. Break each egg into a separate bowl and beat. (1) Add the eggs to the mixture one by one, making sure that each one is completely absorbed before adding the next. If the mixture curdles, add a bit of the flour to make it smooth again. Stir in the lemon juice and rind. Sift the flour and baking powder and add to the mixture. Finally, stir in the milk. (2) Put one third of the mixture into a separate bowl and add the cocoa and extra sugar plus 2 tablespoons of extra milk. Pour half of the light-colored mixture into the cake pan, which you have thoroughly greased with butter in advance. Add the cocoa mixture and finally pour in the remaining light mixture. (3) To increase the marbling effect, you can use a fork to swirl through the dough. Bake the cake for 60 minutes at 375°F. (4) When the cake has cooled a little, turn out onto a wire rack and cover with sifted confectioners sugar. Allow to cool completely before cutting. This cake freezes well.

National specialties

German food does not enjoy as great a reputation as it deserves. As the epithet "Kraut" for a German person – coined in World War I (1914-18) – suggests, people used to think of German food as comprising nothing more varied than *Sauerkraut* and sausages.

Although potatoes, cabbage and sausages have always been staples of the German diet, there is an enormous number of varied recipes in which these foods appear. It is true, for example, that in earlier times people could afford to eat meat only once a week, unless they were

West German butchers take great care in preparing meat for the customer. The sausages, salamis and smoked hams shown here are just a few of the many meats available in West Germany.

very wealthy, so potato-based dishes were central to German cooking. Even though the Germans now eat meat regularly, German cuisine must be unique for its number of different and attractive ways of cooking potatoes. Berliners may have a preference for boiled potatoes, but *Bratkartoffeln* (leftover potatoes sliced and fried with onion) and *Bauernfrühstück* (a hot dish made from leftover potatoes fried with bacon and egg) are just two of the ways in which even boiled potatoes can be dressed up to be more tasty.

The potatoes themselves are sweeter in flavor in Germany than elsewhere. This is due, some say, to the fact that they are left in the ground and only harvested after the first frosts of the autumn. Throughout central Germany, there are endless varieties of *Klösse* or *Knödel* (dumplings), some of them made from a mixture of cooked potato, others from a mixture of raw potato and stale rolls. Add to this the delicious *Kartoffelpuffer* (potato fritters), see page 18, *Kartoffelsalat* (potato salad) and *Kartoffelsuppe* (potato soup), and potatoes seem a great delicacy!

In every butcher's shop in West Germany there hang festoons and garlands of different sausages. *Frankfurter Würstchen*, made from lean pork, are smoked and then simmered. They taste excellent in a lentil, pea or potato soup, as well as with *Sauerkraut* or on their own

Since the Gastarbeiter *came to West Germany in the 1960s, you can find Italian spaghetti houses and Turkish kebab restaurants everywhere.*

with bread and mustard. *Bockwurst* is made from finely ground beef and pork, also smoked, and prepared in the same way as *Frankfurters*. *Bratwürste* are frying and grilling sausages made of pork or veal, and there is nothing so tempting as the smell of *Bratwürste* frying at a sidewalk stand on a cold winter's day. Also served in a roll at such stands are *Currywürste*, which are spicy sausages garnished with a curry-flavored tomato sauce. Just as Germany's central position in Europe has made for a population mix over the centuries, so too has German cooking been subjected to a vast number of influences.

French cooking has been an influential factor since the influx of French Huguenot refugees in the seventeenth century. In the years between World War I and II, the large Jewish population contributed many delicacies. The end of World War II brought thousands of refugees from former German territories in Eastern Europe, who brought their own style of cooking with them. The *Gastarbeiter* (guest workers) who were invited to help run the West German economy in the 1960s and 1970s introduced many interesting styles of cooking. Today there are Greek, Italian and Turkish restaurants and food stores in most West German towns. West German children will tell you that their favorite food is spaghetti or kebabs! Austrian cooking is much famed for its *Schnitzel* (a dish found in every German restaurant and widely thought of as German), goulash, pancakes, *Apfelstrudel* and *Sachertorte* (a rich chocolate cake with a chocolate glaze icing, named after a famous café in Vienna and eaten with dollops of whipped cream). Yet many people would assert that there is no such thing as Austrian cuisine. They claim that what we now know as Austrian food dates from the days of the Austro-Hungarian Empire and is composed mainly of Hungarian and other East European specialties. The internationally relished *Wiener Schnitzel*, for example, originated in the Bohemian woods of what is now Czechoslovakia.

Wiener Schnitzel *is a famous German dish.*

Above *You can buy a wide variety of breads and rolls in West Germany.*

West Germany also lays claim to the greatest variety of breads in the world, with more than 200 types to choose from. Most breads are made from rye flour, rather than the wheat flour used to bake white bread. One of the many bread varieties of Germany that has come onto the international market via America is the *Brezel*, or pretzel as we know it. *Brezeln* are traditionally made of a sourdough yeast mixture and eaten fresh, as a snack with beer.

You can buy Brezeln *(pretzels) at street stands in most West German towns when shopping leaves you hungry for a snack.*

Wiener Schnitzel

(veal cutlet, Vienna-style)

You will need:
4 thin veal or pork (or chicken)
   cutlets
1 egg
salt and pepper
3 tablespoons of flour
7 tablespoons of breadcrumbs
$1/3$ cup of butter, margarine or oil
parsley
lemon wedges or slices

What to do:
(1) Trim any edges of fat off the cutlets with a sharp knife. Press the cutlets down with the flat edge of a large kitchen knife. (2) Place three large plates or soup bowls in a row. In the first, put the flour; in the second, the beaten egg (this can be made to go farther by adding a drop of milk if necessary); and in the third, the breadcrumbs. Rub salt and pepper into both sides of each cutlet (or add the pepper and salt to the flour). (3) Flour each cutlet on both sides, then dip into the egg, and finally coat with breadcrumbs. Place on a board, ready to fry. Heat the butter or oil (or a mixture of both) in the frying pan until it begins to sizzle. If using butter, take care it does not brown. (4) Turn down the heat to medium and fry the *Schnitzel* until they are golden brown and cooked through (about 3–5 minutes on each side). (5) Serve with lemon wedges or slices, mashed potato and green salad.

Safety note:
Ask an adult to help trim the edges of the meat, and be very careful when frying to avoid spitting or burning fat.

Regional specialties

When people eat the internationally known hamburger, few imagine that this meat dish actually came to the world from Hamburg via the United States. The same can be said of the *Frankfurter* – it has become so well known that few people connect it any longer to Frankfurt, its place of origin.

German cooking is extremely rich in regional specialties, and many of them carry the name of the town or district from which they originate. Examples of delicacies that are well known outside the borders of West Germany include *Lübecker* marzipan, *Nürnberger Lebkuchen* (spiced honey cakes) and *Dresdner Christstollen*, the German equivalent of Christmas fruitcake. The German cake perhaps best known internationally is the *Schwarzwälderkirschtorte*, or Black Forest cherry cake, but in West German cafés, this is only one of many equally delicious cakes. Doughnuts

These highly ornamented Lebkuchen *hearts have been inscribed with Valentine's Day messages.*

are very popular in Germany, especially at the time of *Fasching* , or Carnival before Lent. In most of West Germany they are known as *Berliner*, somewhat confusingly, the Berliners themselves call them *Pfannkuchen*, which elsewhere in Germany means pancakes!

Frankfurt "green sauce," a white sauce with many different fresh herbs in it – chives, parsley, tarragon,

A baker holds up the Schwarzwälder-kirschtorte, *a chocolate cake made with cherries, Kirsch liqueur and fresh cream.*

water cress, chervil, sorrel, borage – and served with a pot roast of beef is reputed to have been the favorite dish of Goethe, the most famous German author. Other regional dishes include the famous *Eisbein mit Sauerkraut* from Berlin (knuckles of pork – a fortifying dish for cold winter weather), *Kalbshaxe* (knuckles of veal), known as the national dish of Bavaria, and *Leberkäse* (liver cheese), a cold meat loaf that contains only the slightest trace of liver and no cheese at all! It is made from ground beef, pork and bacon, or *Speck*, and is much enjoyed in Bavaria. The favorite meat dish in Hessen is *Kassler*. This is a loin of pork salted and pickled in brine, then smoked with the addition of juniper berries, which add a very delicate flavor. Rhinelanders prefer *Sauerbraten mit Klössen* (a pot roast of beef, marinated in a spicy, sweet-and-sour sauce and eaten with dumplings). Farther north, there is Westphalian ham, perhaps the best

A plate of delicious Eisbein mit Sauerkraut, *which originated in Berlin, is a popular dish during the cold winters.*

Matjes *herrings, marinated raw herring fillets, were once the staple food of poor fishermen in North Germany, but are now an expensive specialty.*

Below Frikadellen *come from Hamburg, but the recipe for them differs from that for the better-known hamburgers.*

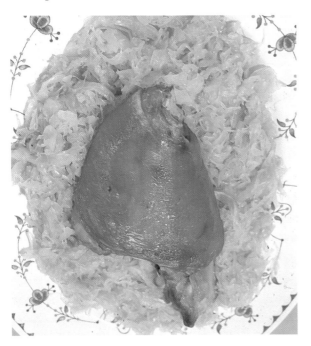

Frickadellen or Bouletten

(Meat patties or hamburgers)

Frikadellen come from Hamburg, *Bouletten* are from Berlin. Unlike American hamburgers, which are all meat, *Frikadellen* and *Bouletten* are mixed with onion, egg and bread, and instead of being grilled, they are fried.

You will need:
1 lb of ground beef
   (or a mixture of beef and pork)
1 stale roll or 1 cup of
   crumbled stale white bread
1 small onion
1 egg, beaten
salt and pepper
1 tablespoon of chopped parsley
   (or chives, thyme or oregano)
butter or oil for frying

What to do:
(1) Soak the bread or roll in the milk until soft. Squeeze out the excess fluid. Beat the egg. (2) Add the bread and the egg to the meat, together with the finely chopped onion, salt, pepper and herbs. Mix well. Mold into a mass with your hands. (3) Take small amounts of the mixture and roll into balls between the palms of your hands. Flatten each ball into a thick patty. (4) Fry the patties slowly in hot butter or oil until well browned (about 7–8 minutes on each side). Serve with potato salad.
Safety note: Take care with the hot oil or butter.

Kartoffelsalat
(potato salad)

You will need:

1½ lb of potatoes   (preferably new
   potatoes)
1 onion
2 tablespoons of oil
2 tablespoons of vinegar
3 tablespoons of mayonnaise or yogurt
salt and pepper
Optional:
½ teaspoon of mustard
dill pickles, sliced
sliced apple

What to do:

(1) Scrub the potatoes and boil them in
their jackets. Peel while still warm, and
dice or slice them. Chop the onion very
fine and mix with the potatoes. (2) Make
the dressing in a separate bowl, adding the
oil and vinegar gradually to thin down the
mayonnaise. Add salt and pepper to taste
and mustard if wished. If the dressing still
seems too thick, thin with a little milk. (3)
Pour the dressing over the potato and
onion and mix well. Let it stand for at least
2 hours and chill before serving. (4)
Garnish with parsley or pickles.

Note:

It is important to have ample dressing as it
soaks into the potatoes.
Tasty additions to the salad are a little fried
bacon, chopped fine, dill pickles sliced, or
sliced fresh apple.

Rote Grüetze
(red fruit pudding)

You will need:
1 lb of red currants
1/2 lb of raspberries
1/2 lb of strawberries
1/2 lb of cherries (optional)
2/3 cup of sugar
1/2 cup of water
1 tablespoon of cornstarch

What to do:
Wash the red currants, raspberries and strawberries and cook for 10 minutes with the sugar and water. Press through a sieve. Mix the cornstarch with 4 tablespoons of cold water to form a smooth paste and stir into the fruit mixture. Bring the mixture to the boil briefly. Add the pitted cherries. Pour immediately into a glass bowl or individual glasses, which have been rinsed with cold water. Chill to set. Serve with unwhipped cream.

Note:
There are many variations on this dish. You can use just some of the fruit, different fruit, or just fruit juice. You can also use tapioca or sago to thicken the dish, in place of the cornstarch. It is often served with custard or milk instead of cream. The dish must be red, and have a sweet-sour taste, so you need red fruits, and some of them should have a tart or sour taste. Failing that, you can use lemon juice to give the pudding its tang.

known of the many smoked hams that have been a German specialty since the days of the Holy Roman Empire. Westphalian ham is made from a boneless piece of pork, which is cured naturally with salt and brine and left to mature for three weeks or so in a cool cellar. It is then smoked over a wood fire until it gains its characteristic dark color and smoky flavor. Westphalian ham is eaten with thickly buttered *Pumpernickel*, which also originally came from Westphalia. *Pumpernickel* is a dark, almost black, rye bread that is baked very slowly and has a strong, slightly sweet flavor.

As accompaniments to these meat dishes, the Swabians much prefer *Spätzle*, a type of handmade pasta, to potatoes. And the white asparagus grown in the Black Forest area is a seasonal delicacy popular throughout Germany and is served with a hollandaise sauce.

Finally, when we reach the sea in Schleswig-Holstein after our culinary trip from south to north, local specialties are all fish dishes. In particular, *Busumer Krabben*, locally caught shrimps, are eaten in salad, as a soup or as a garnish to meat dishes. Herrings were once the staple food of poor people in this region, eaten with boiled potatoes. Today, however, the North Sea is almost fished out; therefore herrings have become a delicacy, as a result of the very strictly imposed fishing quotas. *Bismarckhering*, *Matjes* herrings, herring salad, and rollmops are some of the best-known ways of preparing and eating pickled herrings.

Drinks

German white wines are among the most famous in the world. They grow in a fairly restricted area that represents the most northern, and hence the coolest, grape-growing area in Europe.

The first German vineyards were planted by the Romans two thousand years ago. Today the Rhine and Moselle rivers with their deep,

A hop field in springtime in Bavaria, which prides itself on having the longest tradition in beer brewing.

winding valleys are still home to many vineyards that cling to steep, rocky slopes. These two rivers also give their names to the two best-known wine varieties from Germany.

Rhine wines tend to be slightly sweet and come in brown bottles, whereas Moselle wines are a little drier, and are sold in green bottles. Franconia, where the Rhine and the Main rivers meet, produces the driest German wines, with a refreshing flavor. They come in flask-shaped green bottles.

German wines are identified not only by the shape and color of the bottles in which they are sold. There is also a very precise classification of wines, telling the connoisseur the village where the wine was produced, and the type of grape it was produced from, as well as the year of origin.

Apfelwein (apple wine), or *Ebbelwoi* as it is known in local dialect, is very popular in the Frankfurt area and all over Hessen. It has a tart taste and is traditionally meant to be drunk with *Handkäse mit Musik* (hand cheese with music – small, traditionally handmade, flat balls of cheese, made from curds and matured in an earthenware pot; the "music" is a topping of finely chopped onions, vinegar, oil and a little salt and pepper).

West Germany is, however, better known for its beers than its wines. Germans claim that they have been brewing beer since time immemorial. Certainly they were doing so when the Roman historian Tacitus toured Germania. In 1516 a Purity Law was passed stating that only barley, hops and water could be used in the brewing process. This law still holds, and German brewers are proud of the fact that their beer has no additives in it. Recent EEC pressure on the Germans to import lagers and beers from other member countries, which are not subject to such a law, has not resulted in these beers from outside the country

West Germany is renowned for its white wines, which it exports to many countries; red wine is rarely produced.

A waitress at a typical Bavarian bar in Munich has to have a steady hand to carry so many heavy beer mugs.

flooding the market, as some people first feared.

West Germany is the world's leading exporter of beer. Yet there is no national German beer label. Each town and city still boasts its own local brewery, and beer drinkers tend to patronize their local favorite. This means that there are still a staggering 1,800 breweries in the Federal Republic of West Germany, and the number of different beers they brew among them is something over 5,000!

Bavaria is the regional center for hop growing and beer brewing, and the annual *Oktoberfest* in Munich attracts thousands of international tourists to its beer tents and *Bier Keller* (beer cellars).

Various *Schnaps* (strong liquors), distilled from rye, corn, wheat, oats or barley, are usually drunk straight, alongside beer. Some of them, flavored with juniper, caraway or other herbs, are advertised for their curative properties, particularly as digestive aids. *Weinbrand*, or German brandy, is less well known abroad than the fruit-based brandies, of which the most famous is *Kirsch* or *Kirschwasser*, which is made from cherries.

Somewhat surprisingly, perhaps, given the wealth of wines and beers to choose from, the Germans do not spend their time drinking only alcoholic drinks. Fruit juices

---

Kakao oder Fruchtmilch
(chocolate drink or fruit milkshake)

You will need:
2 cups of milk
1/2 cup of fruit juice or 1 tablespoon of cocoa
sugar to taste

What to do:
Blend the ingredients in a blender or mix well with an egg beater, until frothy.
Note:
If you are mixing milk and fruit juice by hand, beat the milk first until frothy, and add the fruit juice gradually to avoid curdling the milk.
If you are using a blender, make sure the lid is firmly in place before you start, to avoid having a raspberry ceiling in the kitchen!

West Germans drink a lot of pure fruit juices, made from refreshing and unusual blends of wild berries and other fruits.

are extremely popular and are made from a great variety of single fruits or fruit mixtures, for example from apple, pear, red currant, blueberry, cherry and black currant, and many wild berries. Children drink these pure fruit juices in preference to fruit-flavored sodas. Tea, plain or with lemon, is drunk daily by West Germans, and herb teas or fruit-flavored teas are very popular with young people. Coffee is often viewed by outsiders as Germany's national drink. The coffee and cake ritual at home or in the café is an important part of the West German way of life, and the *Kaffeeklatsch*, or chat or gossip over a cup of coffee, is an institution with a very long tradition.

Food and health

Reformierhäuser (literally meaning reform houses!), or health food shops, have existed in Germany throughout this century. The Germans have always had great faith in herbal remedies. A regular feature of the weekly street market is the stand with little sacks of dried herbs lined up on it. Before selling you an herb mixture with which to make an infusion or tea, the seller will ask politely what your ailment is. And almost every German will at some time have visited a "spa" resort town for a health cure. Whether sent by the doctor or having gone voluntarily, West Germans enjoy this enforced rest, and many of

This Reformierhäuser, *or health food store, sells products that many West Germans take to improve their health.*

them return regularly.

In most *Bäder*, or spa towns, like Baden-Baden in the Black Forest or Bad Tölz in Bavaria, natural mineral springs provide the water used in the treatment of various ailments. Not only do they provide the setting for such famous German novels as Thomas Mann's *Zauberberg* (*The Magic Mountain*), these "watering places" are also part of a living tradition. They rely on the belief that diet and exercise, together with the curative properties of the mineral water itself, form an excellent basis for curing a variety of illnesses or for getting the stress of modern living out of one's system.

But spa treatment has not been sufficient to deal with the health problems brought about by the affluence of the West German *Wirtschaftswunder*. In the early 1970s, West Germans became alarmed at the extent of obesity among the population, and at the link between many health problems and a diet too rich in fats, sugar and white flour. Part of the problem was too much meat consumption, which for many Germans in the postwar period had become status symbol of their new prosperity. This was made worse by a tendency to eat pastries

"Taking waters" in Baden-Baden, one of West Germany's most famous spa resorts, is believed to be good for your health.

and cakes with whipped cream every day of the week rather than, as in earlier times, only on special occasions or once a week on Sundays.

The realization of health problems led to the *"Trimm-Dich durch Sport"* ("Get Fit with Sports") campaign, advertised on TV by a small cartoon figure called *Trimmi*. *"Trimm-Dich Pfade"* (fitness trails) were set up in the woods, so loved by the Germans and scene of their pre-coffee and cake Sunday afternoon stroll. Now they changed out of their Sunday best and into their tracksuits, jogging along the trail and pausing only to do push-ups or parallel bar exercises. Many of these trails have fallen into disrepair, having been replaced by a

Two joggers race along a fitness trail in the Black Forest.

more recent fad in fitness, namely gyms and "fitness centers."

Bookshops are full of books and magazines with appetizing color photographs of healthy dishes. Buttermilk, quark, whole-grain bread and the many tasty German vegetable salads are enjoying popularity as a result of this new emphasis on health and fitness. *Vollkornbrot*, whole-grain rye bread, and *Leinsamenbrot*, a coarse wheat bread with seeds from the linseed plant baked into it, are two of the many traditional breads now being promoted by health food stores throughout West Germany.

Kartoffeln mit Kräuter-quark und Gurkensalat

(herb quark with potatoes and cucumber salad)

You will need:
2 lb of potatoes (preferably new
  potatoes)
1/3 cup of quark or yogurt, or yogurt
  mixed with cottage cheese
1 small finely chopped onion, or 3 scallions
4 tablespoons of finely chopped mixed
  herbs (chives, parsley, cress, dill)
salt and pepper
1 large cucumber
2 tablespoons of oil
2 tablespoons of cider or wine vinegar
1/2 teaspoon of salt
milk, as needed for consistency

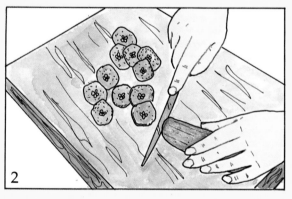

What to do:
Wash the potatoes and boil in salted water
in their jackets. Mix the quark (or yogurt,
etc.) with the milk until it is smooth; add
the chopped onion and herbs. Season with
salt and pepper and put in a serving dish.
Peel the cucumber and slice as thinly as
you can. Sprinkle the sliced cucumber
with salt. Let it stand while you make the
salad dressing, mixing the oil and vinegar.
Pour any excess water off the cucumber
slices before pouring over the dressing.
You can add yogurt or sour cream, and
herbs such as fresh dill to this dressing, but
when serving with the herb quark it may
be better to keep it simple. Arrange the
potatoes, quark and salad on a dinner plate
and serve.

Festive foods

West Germans have a lively sense of tradition and love to celebrate festivals. At Easter, the Easter bunny is an Easter hare in Germany, and he brings colorfully dyed eggs with him. These are hidden indoors or in the backyard, for the children to hunt on Easter morning. Nowadays, children also receive chocolate or marzipan hares and chickens, as well as eggs. Chocolate and hand-painted eggs are arranged together in a basket, where they make a colorful display on the Easter table. Easter decorations include intricately decorated blown eggs from Germany, as well as Scandinavia and Eastern European countries. They are hung from a branch of forsythia or some other spring-flowering shrub set in a vase.

At Christmas time there are many traditions linked with food. The Advent wreath is made at the beginning of December. This is a circle of fir branches wired to a base

Delicately hand-painted and waxed wooden or blown eggs are hung from the branch of a spring-flowering shrub at Easter time.

with four red candles standing in it. One of these is lit every Sunday until Christmas, and this ritual increases the tension and excitement leading up to Christmas. During this period there are always baskets of nuts, oranges and chocolate specialties such as *Dominosteine* (dominoes) in the house. Other Advent and Christmas specialties may include *Lebkuchen* (small, spicy honey cakes, often coated with chocolate), *Spekulatius* (spicy cookies cut into varied shapes) and *Zimtsterne* (cinnamon stars, a type of spicy cookie with a white glazed icing).

When St. Nicholas comes on December 6, he brings nuts and candies to reward good children, but his ugly servant, Ruprecht, comes with a birch rod used to beat naughty children.

When Christmas Eve finally arrives, it is time for the traditional dinner of fresh carp, the fish having been bought live from the fishmonger or the supermarket before being steamed.

Presents are exchanged at afternoon coffee time. On this occasion the *Stollen* – a kind of fruit bread that is the German Christmas fruitcake – is cut. The Christmas tree, with its brightly glowing candles that reflect light off the silver and

A mother and her two children enjoy cups of coffee at Christmas time.

red decorations, has small chocolate figures wrapped in red or silver paper hanging from it.

Traditionally, each member of the family receives *der bunte Teller* (a colorful plate), which is an attractive ceramic or stoneware plate with an abundance of mouth-watering sweet delicacies on it. In earlier times, and especially in large families, this was probably the only present that each child received. Together with shiny polished apples and a great variety of nuts, figs and dates, this plate would contain all the specialty Christmas cookies, and

In this huge festival barn in Munich during the Oktoberfest, *the inscription proclaims Hacker beer to be the "Bavarians' idea of heaven"!*

as a final garnish on top, chocolates, candied fruit and nougat.

Customs involving food are an integral part of most German festivals, whether they be harvest festivals, wine festivals, Carnival or Christmas. You have only to look at the beautiful delicacies on sale at Easter or Christmas to understand just how important these festivals still are in West Germany today.

Marzipankartoffeln

(marzipan balls, or "potatoes," are traditional at Christmas)

You will need:

1¹⁄₃ cups of ground almonds
1¹⁄₃ cups of confectioners sugar
1 egg white, unbeaten
   (from a large egg)
2 teaspoons of orange flower water or
   rosewater (available at drug stores
   or specialty shops)
cocoa

What to do:

Mix the sugar and the almonds well. Add in the egg white and the rosewater or orange flower water. (1) Use a wooden spoon at first, then knead the dough by hand until it has become one soft but firm ball. If it is too stiff, add a little more rosewater or orange flower water. (2) Break off small quantities and roll into small balls (or "potatoes") the size of a marble. (3) When all the balls are formed, roll them in cocoa until they are coated brown. At Christmas time, you can make lovely presents of these marzipan delicacies. Cut out long rectangles of cellophane, fold in half lengthwise and tape the two longer sides to make a transparent bag. You will have enough balls from this recipe to fill about half a dozen bags. (4) Tie the bags at the neck with red yarn or red or green ribbon and you have a present that looks pretty and tastes scrumptiously delicious!

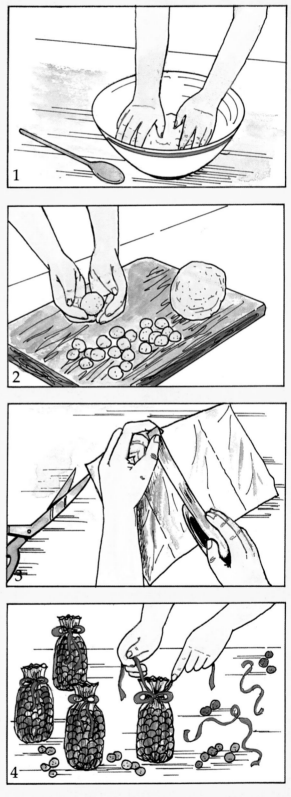

Glossary

Affluence Material wealth.

Allies Britain, France, the United States and the Soviet Union, who fought together to defeat Nazi Germany in World War II.

Animal husbandry Raising animals on a farm for their meat.

Borage A blue-flowered, hairy-leaved plant used in salads and as an herb.

Buttermilk A somewhat acidic milk left after churning butter.

Compote A dish of stewed fruit.

Connoisseur A person of fine judgement in the arts or in matters of taste.

Curative Having the power to cure illness or disease.

Dike An embankment or long turf ridge built up to stop the sea from flooding low-lying farmland.

Earthenware Vessels or pots made of baked clay, often coarse, as opposed to fine porcelain.

EEC The European Economic Community. Often referred to as the Common Market; a collective organization of West European countries, originally set up to ease the flow of trade among them.

Epithet A word or phrase used to characterize a person or thing – often abusive or contemptuous.

Fishing quotas The quantity of fish that individual fishermen or countries may take from the sea under international agreements.

Goulash A very tasty beef or veal stew, originally from Hungary.

Hollandaise sauce A creamy white sauce made with butter, egg yolks and lemon.

Holy Roman Empire The Roman Empire in Western Europe lapsed in 476, but was reestablished in most of what is today Germany by Charlemagne in 800. It existed as the Holy Roman Empire until 1806.

Huguenots French Protestants who fled Catholic France in the sixteenth and seventeenth centuries.

Hypermarket A huge self-service store with a wide range of goods, usually situated on the edge of a town or city.

Migration The movement of people from one country to another, often for economic reasons.

Obesity Fatness; the condition of being seriously overweight.

Quark A cross between yogurt and cottage cheese.

Recession A temporary decline in economic activity or prosperity.

Refugees People seeking refuge in a foreign country, usually fleeing from religious or political persecution, sometimes from war, or from natural disasters such as earthquakes.

Republic A society in which the supreme power is held by elected government representatives, headed by a president, rather than a king or queen.

Sauerkraut A German dish of chopped pickled cabbage, available in supermarkets.

Self-sufficient Producing all that one requires, needing to buy or import nothing.

Staple food Principal element in a diet.

Stereotype An unduly fixed and often repeated idea of how things or people are.

German words and phrases

General

Guten Tag Hello, good day
Guten Abend Good evening
Gute Nacht Good night
Auf Wiedersehen Goodbye
Bitte Please
Danke schön Thank you
Wie geht es Ihnen? How are you
Danke, es geht mir gut. Good, thanks.
Wie heissen Sie? What's your name?
Ich heisse Silke. My name is Silke.
Wo wohnen Sie? Where do you live?
Ich wohne in Hannover. I live in Hannover.
Ich möchte... I'd like...
Was kostet das? How much is that?
Wo ist...? Where is...?
Entschuldigen Sie mich. Excuse me.
Wieviel Uhr ist es? What is the time?

At the restaurant

Ich möchte einen Tisch für zwei, bitte, für halb eins.
I'd like a table for two, please, for 12:30.
Die Speisekarte, bitte.
Please may I have the menu.
Ich habe grossen Hunger
I'm very hungry.
Ich habe auch Durst.
I'm thirsty too.
Was möchten Sie essen/trinken?
What would you like to eat/drink?
Ich möchte bitte einen Wiener Schnitzel/die Gulaschuppe/ Sauerbraten mit Pommes frites/ Bratkartoffeln/Klössen und einen grünen Salat.
I'd like *Wiener Schnizel/* goulash soup/sweet-and-sour pot roast with french fries/sauté potatoes/potato dumplings and a green salad, please.

Haben Sie einen trockenen Weisswein/Apfelsaft, bitte?
Have you a dry white wine/ any apple juice, please?
Guten Appetit!
Enjoy your meal!
Die Rechnung, bitte.
The bill, please.

die Torte pastry
die Obsttorte fruit tart
der Tee tea
der Kaffee coffee
das Mineralwasser mineral water
der (Apfel)saft (apple) juice
der Wein wine
das Bier beer

Food

Das Brot/das Brötchen
Bread / roll
die Butter butter
die Wurst sausage
der Käse cheese
das Ei egg
das Fleisch meat
Schweinefleisch/Kalbfleisch
pork / veal
das Gemüse vegetables
die Kartoffeln potatoes
die Tomaten tomatoes
der Kohl/das Kraut cabbage
die Karotten/Möhren carrots
die Erbsen peas
der Salat salad, lettuce
das Obst fruit
der Kuchen cake

Acknowledgments
The author would like to thank Ester Einhorn for a childhood full of delicious German food, and Ben Evans and Herta Kleiser for their help in putting together this book.

Picture acknowledgments
The publisher would like to thank the following people for providing photographs for this book: Andy Hasson: 4,5,6,7,8,9,10, 11,12,13,14,15(both),16,17(both), 22, 23, 24, 25 (both), 27, 28, 29(top and bottom), 33, 34, 35, 36, 37, 38, 39, 41; Zefa: 7,42,43. The map on page 5 is by Malcolm S. Walker.

Further reading list

Around the World in Eighty Dishes by Polly and Tasha Van der Linde, Scroll Press.
Betty Crocker's Cookbook for Boys and Girls by Western Publ., 1984.
Christmas Cooking Around the World by Susan Pardy, Franklin Watts, 1983.

Follow the Sun: International Cooking for Young People by Mary Deming and Joyce Haddard, Sun Scope, 1982.
Let's Look Up Food From Many Lands by Beverly Birch, Silver Burdett, 1985.
Wide World Cookbook by Rebecca Shapiro, Little, Brown & Co., 1962.

Index